APA MANUAL
SEVENTH EDITION 2023

Crafting Excellence in Academic Writing

SEVENTH EDITION

APA MANUAL

Crafting Citations and Style, Writing Excellence and Scholarly Pursuits to Academic Success

JOHN STEWORT

Table of Contents

A

Abbreviations and Acronyms

   - Guidelines for use

   - Examples:

     - APA (American Psychological Association)

     - DOI (Digital Object Identifier)

     - et al. (et alia, meaning "and others")

     - etc. (et cetera, meaning "and so forth")

Abstract

   - Purpose and structure

   - Length requirements

   - Key components

B

Bias-Free Language

   - Strategies for avoiding bias

   - Gender-neutral language

- Guidelines for inclusive writing

Citations and References

- In-text citations
  - Author-date format
  - Page numbers
  - Citing multiple works
- Reference list entries
  - Book references
  - Journal article references
  - Website references
- Formatting rules
  - Italics and capitalization
  - Punctuation

Data

- Reporting statistics
  - Descriptive statistics
  - Inferential statistics
- Tables and figures
  - Guidelines for creation
  - Placement and formatting

- APA tables and figures
    - Examples and templates

Ethical Principles
- Informed consent
    - Definition and importance
    - Guidelines for obtaining consent
- Research with vulnerable populations
    - Definitions and considerations
    - Guidelines for ethical research

F

Figures and Tables
- Creating and formatting
    - Design principles
    - APA guidelines for figures and tables
- Legends and notes
    - Explanation of terms
    - Placement and formatting
- Lists of tables and figures
    - Guidelines for organization

- Formatting requirements

G

Grammar and Usage

- Punctuation
  - Commas, semicolons, and colons
  - Use of parentheses and brackets
- Verb tense
  - Guidelines for consistent tense usage
  - Shifting tenses in academic writing

I

In-Text Citations

- Author-date format
  - Single and multiple authors
  - Group authors
- Quoting and paraphrasing
  - Rules for direct quotations
  - Strategies for effective paraphrasing

J

Journal Article Reporting Standards

- Overview of reporting standards

- Guidelines for reporting different types of research studies

L

Lists

- Bulleted and numbered lists

  - Proper use and formatting

- Capitalization and punctuation

  - Guidelines for consistent styling

M

Mathematics and Statistics

- Mathematical symbols

  - Proper use and formatting

- Reporting statistics

  - Guidelines for presenting statistical data

P

Paper Format
- Title page
  - Author information
  - Title format
- Abstract
  - Guidelines for writing
  - Length and content
- Headings
  - Levels of headings
  - Formatting guidelines
- Lists
  - Guidelines for creating and formatting lists
- Appendices
  - Proper use and formatting guidelines

Plagiarism
- Definition and types of plagiarism
- Strategies for avoiding plagiarism
- Proper citation practices

Quotations
- Short and long quotations
  - Rules for incorporating quotes
  - Formatting guidelines
- Block quotations
  - Guidelines for formatting and indenting

R

Reference Entries
- Books
  - Examples and formatting guidelines
- Journal articles
  - Examples and formatting guidelines
- Websites
  - Examples and formatting guidelines

Research Methods
- Experimental design
  - Guidelines for describing research design
- Qualitative research
  - Guidelines for reporting qualitative studies

Style and Tone

- Clarity and conciseness
  - Strategies for clear writing
- Formal writing
  - Guidelines for maintaining a formal tone

Title Page

- Author information
  - Proper formatting of author names
- Title format
  - Guidelines for title styling

Writing Style

- Active voice
  - Advantages and guidelines for using active voice
- Verb tense
  - Consistent use of verb tenses
  - Shifting tenses in academic writing

V

Visual Elements

- Tables and figures

    - Guidelines for creating and formatting

- Captions and notes

    - Guidelines for writing captions and notes

Vulnerable Populations

- Definition and examples

- Guidelines for conducting research with vulnerable populations

Introduction

Crafting Excellence in Academic Writing with APA Manual 7th Edition

Welcome to the realm of scholarly writing, where precision and clarity reign supreme. As aspiring academics and seasoned researchers alike navigate the intricate landscape of academic discourse, a reliable guide becomes an indispensable companion. In this pursuit of excellence, the "APA Manual 7th Edition" stands as a beacon, offering a comprehensive set of rules and guidelines that shape the very fabric of academic communication.

This book serves as your gateway to mastering the art of academic writing, unveiling strategies and techniques intricately woven with the insights of the APA Manual 7th Edition. Whether you are a student working on your first research paper or a seasoned researcher aiming for publication, the journey to writing excellence begins here.

Join us on a comprehensive exploration that demystifies the intricacies of APA style, from the meticulous construction of citations to the artful presentation of visual elements. We delve into the nuances of creating and formatting tables and figures, understanding the delicate balance of style and tone, and addressing ethical considerations in research with vulnerable populations.

Each chapter unfolds a new facet of academic writing, incorporating the wisdom embedded in the pages of the APA Manual 7th Edition. From the basics of reference entries for diverse sources to the subtleties of maintaining a formal tone, this guide is designed to empower you with the knowledge and skills needed to navigate the rigorous landscape of academic communication.

Embark on this journey with us as we unravel the intricacies of scholarly writing, armed with the invaluable insights encapsulated in the APA Manual 7th Edition. Your pursuit of academic excellence starts here, where words become a powerful vessel for ideas, and precision becomes the hallmark of your scholarly endeavors

A
Abbreviations and Acronyms

- **Guidelines for Use:**
  - **Introduction:**
    - Abbreviations and acronyms should be used sparingly and only when necessary to enhance comprehension.
    - Always consider the clarity and readability of the text when deciding whether to use an abbreviation.

  - **First Use Rule:**
    - Spell out the full term or phrase followed by the abbreviation/acronym in parentheses the first time it appears in the text.
    - Example: The American Psychological Association (APA) provides guidelines for academic writing.

  - **Subsequent Use:**
    - Use the abbreviation/acronym alone in subsequent references.
    - Example: APA style is commonly used in the social sciences.

- **Exceptions:**
  - Commonly used abbreviations (e.g., USA, NATO) and those well-known in a particular field might not require spelled-out introduction.

Examples:

1. **APA**: American Psychological Association
   - *First Use*: The guidelines provided by the American Psychological Association (APA)...
   - *Subsequent Use*: APA style is widely accepted.

2. **DOI**: Digital Object Identifier
   - *First Use*: The article is identified by its Digital Object Identifier (DOI).
   - *Subsequent Use*: The DOI simplifies referencing.

3. **et al.**: et alia (and others)
   - *First Use*: The research team (Smith et al., 2020) found...
   - *Subsequent Use*: Smith et al. (2020) conducted a comprehensive study.

4. **etc.**: et cetera (and so forth)
   - *First Use*: The lab equipment includes microscopes, test tubes, etc.

- *Subsequent Use*: Ensure proper handling of chemicals, glassware, etc.

Abstract

Purpose and Structure:

- **Purpose:**
  - The abstract provides a concise summary of the research paper, conveying the purpose, methodology, results, and conclusion.
  - It serves as a standalone description of the study.

- **Structure:**
  - Typically, structured into four parts: Introduction, Method, Results, and Conclusion.
  - Each part includes key information without excessive detail.

Length Requirements:

- **Word Count:**
  - Generally, abstracts should be between 150 to 250 words.
  - Check the specific requirements of the journal or assignment, as word count limits may vary.

- **Conciseness**:
    - Be concise but include essential information.
    - Avoid unnecessary details or background information.

Key Components:

1. Introduction:
  - Briefly state the research problem or question.
  - Include the purpose or objective of the study.

2. Method:
  - Describe the research design, participants, materials, and procedures.
  - Provide enough detail for readers to understand the study's methodology.

3. Results:
  - Summarize the main findings.
  - Avoid interpretation; focus on factual results.

4. Conclusion:
  - Present the study's implications and potential applications.
  - Avoid new information; summarize the significance of the findings.

Example:

- *Example Abstract:*

This study examines the impact of mindfulness meditation on stress reduction in college students. Participants (N=100) engaged in a 4-week mindfulness program. Results indicated a significant decrease in self-reported stress levels (p < 0.05). These findings suggest that mindfulness interventions can be effective in reducing stress among college students.

B

Bias-Free Language

Strategies for Avoiding Bias:

- **Use of Gender-Neutral Language:**

  - Replace gendered terms with neutral ones.

    - Example: Instead of "policeman," use "police officer."

  - Use singular "they" when gender is unknown or irrelevant.

    - Example: The student completed their assignment.

- **Avoiding Stereotypes:**

  - Be cautious with language reinforcing stereotypes.

    - Example: Avoid assuming gender roles in descriptions (e.g., "nurses are nurturing").

- **Inclusive Writing:**

  - Consider diverse perspectives and experiences.

    - Example: Use terms like "partner" instead of assuming marital status.

Citations and References

In-Text Citations:

- **Author-Date Format:**
  - Identify the source with the author's last name and the publication year.
    - Example: (Smith, 2019)
  - For direct quotes, include page numbers.
    - Example: (Smith, 2019, p. 42)

- **Citing Multiple Works:**
  - Differentiate between multiple sources.
    - Example: (Smith, 2019; Johnson, 2020)

Reference List Entries:

- **Book References:**
  - Include the author's name, publication year, book title, and publisher.
    - Example: Smith, J. (2019). The Art of Writing. Publisher.

- **Journal Article References:**
  - Include the author's name, publication year, article title, journal name, volume, issue, page range.

- Example: Johnson, M. (2020). Research in Action. *Journal of Science*, 5(2), 120-135.

- **Website References:**
  - Include the author's name (if available), publication date, page title, website name, and URL.
  - Example: World Health Organization. (2020). COVID-19 Guidelines. [URL]

- **Formatting Rules:**
  - **Italics and Capitalization:**
    - Italicize book and journal titles.
      - Example: *The Journal of Psychology.*
    - Capitalize the first word of the title and subtitle.
      - Example: *Psychology Today: An Overview.*

  - **Punctuation:**
    - End each reference with a period.
    - Use a hanging indent for each line after the first in a reference entry.

Data

Reporting Statistics:

- **Descriptive Statistics:**

  - Summarize and describe the main features of a dataset.

    - Example: Mean and standard deviation were calculated for each variable.

- **Inferential Statistics:**

  - Make inferences and predictions about a population based on a sample.

    - Example: The results were statistically significant ($p < 0.05$).

Tables and Figures:

- **Guidelines for Creation:**

  - Clearly label and title tables and figures.

    - Example: Table 1: Descriptive Statistics of Participants.

- **Placement and Formatting:**

    - Place tables and figures as close as possible to the text referring to them.

    - Ensure clarity and readability.

- **APA Tables and Figures:**
  - Follow specific guidelines for formatting APA tables and figures.
    - Example: Refer to APA Manual for detailed templates and examples.

Ethical Principles

Informed Consent:

- **Definition and Importance:**
  - Informed consent involves providing participants with information about the study's purpose, procedures, risks, and benefits.
    - Example: Participants were informed about the study and provided written consent.

- **Guidelines for Obtaining Consent:**
  - Clearly explain the study, allowing participants to make an informed decision.
    - Example: A consent form detailing the study's purpose and procedures was presented to each participant.

Research with Vulnerable Populations:

- **Definitions and Considerations:**

  - Vulnerable populations include those who may be at risk or lack the capacity to provide fully informed consent.

    - Example: Children, prisoners, and individuals with cognitive impairments are considered vulnerable.

- **Guidelines for Ethical Research:**

  - Extra precautions are necessary when conducting research with vulnerable populations.

    - Example: Additional steps were taken to ensure the well-being and understanding of participants in the vulnerable group.

Figures and Tables

Creating and Formatting:

- **Design Principles:**
  - **Clarity and Simplicity:**
    - Figures and tables should be designed for clarity, simplicity, and ease of understanding.
      - Example: A bar graph visually representing the relationship between variables should have clear axes labels and legends.

  - **Consistency:**
    - Maintain consistent formatting throughout figures and tables for a professional appearance.
      - Example: Use the same font, size, and style for all text elements in a table.

- **APA Guidelines for Figures and Tables:**
  - **Titles and Captions:**
    - Each figure and table should have a concise, informative title.
      - Example: Figure 1: Distribution of Survey Responses.

- Provide a caption explaining the content or context.
  - Example: Figure 1. Distribution of Survey Responses by Age Group.

- **Numbering:**
  - Number figures and tables separately, in the order they are mentioned in the text.
    - Example: Table 2 presents demographic information for the study participants.

- **References:**
  - Cite the source of the figure or table if not original.
    - Example: Adapted from "Title of Source," by Author, Year, Journal Title, Volume, p. xx. Copyright [Year] by Copyright Holder.

- **Legends and Notes:**
  - **Explanation of Terms:**
    - Clearly define any abbreviations or symbols used in the figure or table.
      - Example: Note: SD = Standard Deviation.

- **Placement and Formatting:**
  - Place legends (explanatory information) and notes (additional details) below the figure or table.
    - Example: Note: Data represents mean values; error bars indicate standard deviation.

- **Lists of Tables and Figures:**
  - **Guidelines for Organization:**
    - Include a separate list of tables and a list of figures after the table of contents.
    - Example: List of Tables

      Table 1. Demographic Information

      Table 2. Results of Statistical Analysis

      List of Figures

      Figure 1. Distribution of Responses

      Figure 2. Comparison of Groups

  - **Formatting Requirements:**
    - Format the list entries with the same font and spacing as the rest of the document.
    - Example: List of Tables and Figures should be double-spaced with a consistent font throughout.

G

Grammar and Usage

Punctuation:

- **Commas, Semicolons, and Colons:**
  - **Commas:**
    - Use commas to separate items in a series.
      - Example: The study included participants from diverse backgrounds, ages, and occupations.
    - Use commas before coordinating conjunctions in compound sentences.
      - Example: The results were inconclusive, but further research is warranted.

  - **Semicolons:**
    - Use semicolons to separate items in a series when the items themselves contain commas.
      - Example: The participants included individuals from New York, New York; Los Angeles, California; and Chicago, Illinois.
    - Use semicolons to connect independent clauses without a conjunction.

- Example: The experiment was successful; however, more data are needed.

- **Colons:**

  - Use colons to introduce a list or to emphasize a clause.

    - Example: The survey measured several factors: age, income, and education.

  - Use colons to introduce a statement that explains or follows from the first part.

    - Example: The conclusion is clear: more research is needed.

- **Use of Parentheses and Brackets:**
  - **Parentheses:**

    - Use parentheses for supplementary, nonessential information.

      - Example: The results (which were unexpected) suggest a need for further investigation.

    - Avoid using parentheses for essential information; use commas instead.

      - Incorrect: The participants (from the control group) were excluded.

  - **Brackets:**

    - Use brackets to enclose editorial comments or explanations within quoted material.

- Example: "The participants [in the study] reported increased satisfaction."

Verb Tense:

- **Guidelines for Consistent Tense Usage:**
  - Maintain a consistent verb tense within a section or paragraph.
    - Example: The study investigates the effects of climate change on biodiversity. The researchers analyze data from multiple regions.

  - Choose past tense to describe completed actions and findings in the study.
    - Example: The experiment concluded with statistically significant results.

  - Use present tense for general truths and established knowledge.
    - Example: Newton's laws of motion state that an object at rest tends to stay at rest.

- **Shifting Tenses in Academic Writing:**
  - Avoid unnecessary shifts in tense unless there is a clear reason.

- Example: The literature review presents studies on the topic. The researcher conducted an experiment to further explore the phenomenon.

- Use past tense to describe the methods and results of the study.
  - Example: The participants were randomly assigned to groups, and the data were analyzed using statistical software.

- Use present tense for statements that are universally true.
  - Example: The introduction outlines the purpose of the study and presents relevant background information.

In-Text Citations

Author-Date Format:

- **Single and Multiple Authors:**
  - **Single Author:**

   - Include the author's last name and the publication year.

      - Example: (Smith, 2018)

   - If the author's name is part of the sentence, only include the publication year in parentheses.

      - Example: According to Smith (2018),...

  - **Multiple Authors:**

   - For two authors, use an ampersand (&) between their names.

      - Example: (Johnson & Miller, 2019)

   - For three or more authors, list the first author followed by "et al." (meaning "and others").

      - Example: (Anderson et al., 2020)

  - **Group Authors:**

   - Use the full name of the group as the author.

- Example: (American Psychological Association, 2017)
- If the abbreviation is well-known, include it in square brackets for the first citation and use it in subsequent citations.
- Example: (APA, 2017)

Quoting and Paraphrasing:

- **Rules for Direct Quotations:**
  - **Short Quotations (Less than 40 words):**

  - Integrate the quote into the text and enclose it in double quotation marks.
  - Example: According to Smith (2018), "The results indicated a significant correlation between the variables" (p. 42).
  - Include the author, year, and page number in the citation.

  - **Long Quotations (40 words or more):**

  - Start the quote on a new line, indented 0.5 inches from the left margin.
  - Omit quotation marks, and include the author, year, and page number in parentheses at the end.
  - Example:

    The study found that:

    ... (Smith, 2018, p. 42).

- **Strategies for Effective Paraphrasing:**
  - **Understand the Original:**

    - Grasp the meaning of the original text before attempting to paraphrase.

  - **Use Different Words and Sentence Structure:****

    - Express the information in your own words and sentence structure.
      - Original: "The experiment demonstrated a clear cause-and-effect relationship."
      - Paraphrased: "The study illustrated a definite relationship between cause and effect."

  - **Cite the Source:**

    - Even when paraphrasing, provide an in-text citation to credit the original source.
      - Example: (Smith, 2018)

  - **Check for Plagiarism:**

    - Ensure that your paraphrased text is sufficiently different from the original to avoid unintentional plagiarism.

J

Journal Article Reporting Standards

Overview of Reporting Standards:

- **Purpose:**
  - Reporting standards ensure consistency and transparency in the presentation of research findings in journal articles.

- **Standard Elements:**
  - Articles should include standard elements such as title, abstract, introduction, methods, results, discussion, and references.

- **Transparent Reporting:**
  - Encourages clear and complete reporting of study details for the benefit of readers and future researchers.

- **Compliance:**
  - Journals often require authors to adhere to specific reporting standards to facilitate peer review and reproducibility.

Guidelines for Reporting Different Types of Research Studies:

- **Experimental Studies:**
  - **Overview:**
    - Experimental studies involve manipulating variables to observe the effect on outcomes.
  - **Guidelines:**
    - Clearly describe the experimental design, including variables, procedures, and randomization.
    - Example: "A between-subjects experimental design was employed, with participants randomly assigned to either the control or experimental group."

- **Observational Studies:**
  - **Overview:**
    - Observational studies involve observing and recording behavior without intervention.
  - **Guidelines:**
    - Detail the observational methods, such as naturalistic or structured observation.
    - Example: "This observational study used a naturalistic approach, with researchers observing participants in their natural environment."

- **Survey Research:**
  - **Overview:**
    - Survey research involves collecting data through questionnaires or interviews.
  - **Guidelines:**
    - Describe the survey instrument, sampling method, and response rate.
    - Example: "A Likert scale was used in a cross-sectional survey, with a response rate of 75%."

- **Meta-Analyses:**
  - **Overview:**
    - Meta-analyses involve synthesizing data from multiple studies to draw conclusions.
  - **Guidelines:**
    - Clearly outline the inclusion criteria for studies, statistical methods used, and results.
    - Example: "This meta-analysis included studies published between 2010 and 2020, using a random-effects model to combine effect sizes."

- **Qualitative Studies:**
  - **Overview:**
    - Qualitative studies explore experiences, meanings, and perspectives.

- **Guidelines:**
  - Provide a detailed description of the qualitative approach, data collection, and data analysis methods.
  - Example: "This phenomenological study employed in-depth interviews and thematic analysis to explore participants' lived experiences."

Additional Considerations:

- **Ethical Considerations:**
  - Emphasize ethical considerations, including informed consent, protection of participants, and disclosure of conflicts of interest.

- **Limitations:**
  - Acknowledge and discuss study limitations to provide a balanced interpretation of results.

- **Generalizability:**
  - Clearly state the extent to which findings can be generalized to other populations or contexts.

L

Lists

Bulleted and Numbered Lists:

- **Proper Use and Formatting:**
  - **Bulleted Lists:**
    - Use bulleted lists to present items in no particular order.
      - Example:
        - Item 1
        - Item 2
        - Item 3

  - **Numbered Lists:**
    - Use numbered lists for items that follow a sequence or hierarchy.
      - Example:
        1. First item
        2. Second item
        3. Third item

- **Capitalization and Punctuation:**
  - **Guidelines for Consistent Styling:**
    - Maintain consistent capitalization and punctuation within lists.
      - Example:
        - Begin each item with a capital letter.
        - End each item with a period if it's a complete sentence.

    - First item.
    - Second item.
    - Third item.

    1. First item.
    2. Second item.
    3. Third item.

M

Mathematics and Statistics

Mathematical Symbols

- **Proper Use and Formatting:**
  - **Symbols:**
    - Use standard mathematical symbols for clarity.
      - Example: α+β=γ
  - **Equations:**
    - Format equations consistently and provide explanations if necessary.
    - Example: The formula for calculating variance is $s^2 = \frac{\sum(X-\bar{X})^2}{n-1}$

Reporting Statistics:

- **Guidelines for Presenting Statistical Data:**
  - **Descriptive Statistics:**
    - Clearly present mean, median, standard deviation, etc.
      - Example: The mean age of participants was 35.2 years (SD = 5.8).

- **Inferential Statistics:**
  - Include p-values and confidence intervals for hypothesis testing.
    - Example: The results were statistically significant ($p<0.05$).

- **Effect Sizes:**
  - Report effect sizes for the magnitude of differences.
    - Example: Cohen's d was 0.75, indicating a medium effect size.

- **Tables and Figures:**
  - Use tables and figures for complex statistical data.
    - Example: Refer to Table 1 for a summary of descriptive statistics.

- **APA Tables and Figures:**
  - Follow specific guidelines for formatting APA tables and figures.
    - Example: See APA Manual for detailed templates and examples.

P

Paper Format

Title Page:

- **Author Information:**

    - Include the author's name, affiliation (if applicable), and author note (optional).

        - Example:

        John A. Smith

        Department of Psychology, University of XYZ

        Author Note: This research was supported by a grant from...

- **Title Format:**

    - The title should be concise and clearly reflect the main idea of the paper.

    - Example:

        ```

        The Impact of Mindfulness Meditation on Stress Reduction in College Students

        ```

- **Abstract:**

  - **Guidelines for Writing:**
    - Provide a concise summary of the research paper.
    - Include the purpose, methods, results, and conclusions.
      - Example:

        This study examines the effects of a 4-week mindfulness meditation program on stress levels in college students. Participants...

  - **Length and Content:**
    - Typically, the abstract should be between 150 to 250 words.
    - Avoid including unnecessary details or references.
      - Example:

        Results indicated a significant reduction in self-reported stress levels ($p < 0.05$). These findings suggest that mindfulness interventions...

Headings:

- **Levels of Headings:**
  - **Level 1:**
    - Centered, bold, and title case.
    - Example: **Introduction**

- **Level 2:**
  - Flush left, bold, and title case.
    - Example: **Literature Review**
- **Level 3:**
  - Indented, bold, and sentence case, ending with a period.
    - Example: *Research Design.*

- **Formatting Guidelines:**
  - Use consistent formatting throughout the document.
  - Ensure that each level of heading is distinct and clearly indicates the hierarchy.
    - Example:

      Method

      Participants.

      Sample.

- **Lists:**

  - **Guidelines for Creating and Formatting Lists:**
    - Use bulleted lists for items without a particular order and numbered lists for sequences.
    - Ensure consistent indentation and punctuation.
      - Example:

- Item 1

- Item 2

- Item 3

```

1. First item

2. Second item

3. Third item

**Appendices:**

- **Proper Use and Formatting Guidelines:**
  - Include supplementary materials that are too lengthy for the main text.
  - Label each appendix with a letter (e.g., Appendix A) and provide a title.
    - Example:

      Appendix A: Survey Questions

  - **Format for Appendices**:
    - Ensure each appendix is formatted consistently.
    - Include relevant details, such as tables or figures.
      - Example:
```

Table A1: Demographic Information

Plagiarism

Definition and Types of Plagiarism:

- **Definition:**
  - Plagiarism is the act of presenting someone else's ideas, words, or work as your own without proper acknowledgment.

- **Types of Plagiarism:**
  - **Copy-and-Paste Plagiarism:**
    - Directly copying and pasting text without quotation marks or citation.
  - **Paraphrasing Plagiarism:**
    - Rewriting someone else's work without proper citation.
  - **Patchwriting:**
    - Using a mix of copied and original phrases without appropriate attribution.

- **Self-Plagiarism:**
    - Presenting one's own previously published work without citation.

Strategies for Avoiding Plagiarism:

- **Proper Citation Practices:**
    - Cite all sources used in your research, including direct quotes, paraphrased information, and ideas.
        - Example: According to Smith (2018), "quoting directly from a source requires proper citation" (p. 42).

- **Quoting and Paraphrasing:**
    - Use quotation marks for verbatim text and provide a citation.
        - Example: The author states, "In-text citations are crucial in avoiding plagiarism" (Jones, 2019, p. 30).
    - Paraphrase by rephrasing the information in your own words and citing the source.

- **Manage Your Time:**
    - Plan your research and writing process to avoid last-minute pressures that may lead to unintentional plagiarism.

- **Use Plagiarism Detection Tools:**
  - Utilize plagiarism detection tools to scan your work for unintentional similarities with existing content.

Q

Quotations

Short and Long Quotations:

- **Rules for Incorporating Quotes:**
  - **Short Quotations (Less than 40 words):**
    - Integrate the quote into the text with double quotation marks.
    - Example: According to Smith (2018), "In-text citations are crucial in avoiding plagiarism" (p. 42).

  - **Long Quotations (40 words or more):**
    - Start the quote on a new line, indented 0.5 inches from the left margin, without quotation marks.
    - Maintain double spacing.
    - Example:
      > **The author contends that:**
      > **"In-text citations play a pivotal role in scholarly writing, ensuring proper attribution and academic integrity" (Jones, 2019, p. 55).**

- **Formatting Guidelines:**
  - **Punctuation:**
    - Place commas and periods inside quotation marks.
    - Example: According to Brown (2020), "APA style is widely used in academic writing."

  - **Ellipses:**
    - Use ellipses (...) to indicate omitted words from a quote.
    - Example: The author notes, "In-text citations ... serve to acknowledge the source" (Smith, 2018, p. 23).

Block Quotations:

- **Guidelines for Formatting and Indenting:**
  - Use block quotations for quotes longer than 40 words.
  - Start the quote on a new line, indented 0.5 inches from the left margin.
  - Example:

    The research findings highlight the significance of in-text citations in academic writing. According to Smith (2018),

    ...

    acknowledging the source is fundamental for maintaining academic integrity (p. 42).

R

Reference Entries

Books:

- **Examples and Formatting Guidelines:**
  - **Single Author:**
    - Last name, Initials. (Year). *Title of the book*. Publisher.
    - Example: Smith, J. (2019). *The Art of Writing*. ABC Publishers.

  - **Two Authors:**
    - Last name, Initials., & Last name, Initials. (Year). *Title of the book*. Publisher.
    - Example: Johnson, M., & Brown, A. (2020). *Research Methods*. XYZ Press.

  - **Multiple Authors (Up to 20):**
    - List all authors in the reference entry.
    - Example: Anderson, L., et al. (2021). *Advanced Statistics*. Research Books.

Journal Articles:

- **Examples and Formatting Guidelines:**
  - **Print Journal Article:**
    - Last name, Initials. (Year). Title of the article. *Title of the Journal*, Volume(Issue), Page range.
      - Example: Smith, J. (2018). Writing techniques in modern literature. *Journal of Creative Writing*, 5(2), 120-135.

  - **Online Journal Article with DOI:**
    - Last name, Initials. (Year). Title of the article. *Title of the Journal*, Volume(Issue), Page range. DOI
      - Example: Johnson, M. (2019). The impact of technology on education. *Journal of Educational Technology*, 8(3), 210-225. https://doi.org/xxxxx

  - **Online Journal Article without DOI:**
    - Last name, Initials. (Year). Title of the article. *Title of the Journal*, Volume(Issue), Page range. URL
      - Example: Brown, A. (2020). Trends in environmental conservation. *Environmental Science Journal*, 15(4), 330-345. https://www.journalurl.com

Websites:

- **Examples and Formatting Guidelines:**
  - **Webpage with an Author:**
    - Last name, Initials. (Year, Month Day). Title of the webpage. *Name of the Website*. URL
    - Example: Smith, J. (2021, June 15). Writing tips for effective communication. *Writer's Hub*. https://www.writershub.com/tips

  - **Webpage without an Author:**
    - Title of the webpage. (Year, Month Day). *Name of the Website*. URL
    - Example: APA Citation Guide. (2022, January 5). *APA Style*. https://www.apastyle.org

Research Methods

Experimental Design

- **Guidelines for Describing Research Design:**
    - Clearly describe the experimental design used in the study.
        - Example: The study employed a randomized controlled trial design, with participants randomly assigned to either the experimental or control group.

Qualitative Research

- **Guidelines for Reporting Qualitative Studies:**
    - Provide a detailed description of the qualitative approach, data collection methods, and data analysis procedures.
        - Example: This qualitative study utilized a phenomenological approach, conducting in-depth interviews to explore participants' lived experiences. Thematic analysis was then applied to identify recurring patterns in the data.

S

Style and Tone

Clarity and Conciseness:

- **Strategies for Clear Writing:**
  - **Use Plain Language:**
    - Express ideas in straightforward and clear language.
      - Example: Instead of "utilize," use "use."
  - **Avoid Ambiguity:**
    - Clearly convey your message without leaving room for misinterpretation.
      - Example: Ambiguous - "The results may possibly indicate a trend." Clear - "The results suggest a trend."
  - **Organize Information:**
    - Present information logically, using clear and structured organization.
      - Example: Use headings and subheadings to organize content.

Formal Writing:

- **Guidelines for Maintaining a Formal Tone:**
  - **Avoid Colloquialisms:**
    - Refrain from using informal expressions or slang.
      - Example: Instead of "a lot," use "many" or "numerous."

  - **Use Third Person:**
    - Write in the third person to maintain objectivity.
      - Example: Instead of "I found," use "The study found."

  - **Eliminate Contractions:**
    - Write out contractions to maintain formality.
      - Example: Instead of "can't," use "cannot."

Title Page

Author Information:

- **Proper Formatting of Author Names:**
  - List authors' names with their first name, middle initial (if applicable), and last name.
    - Example: John A. Smith

Title Format:

- **Guidelines for Title Styling:**
  - Use title case for the main title (capitalize the first letter of each major word).
    - Example: *The Impact of Climate Change on Biodiversity*

  - Keep the title concise but informative.
    - Example: *Exploring the Role of Social Media in Adolescent Mental Health*

Writing Style

Active Voice:

- **Advantages and Guidelines for Using Active Voice:**
  - **Advantages:**
    - Promotes clarity and directness.
    - Emphasizes the doer of the action.

  - **Guidelines:**
    - Place the subject of the sentence before the action.

- Example: Passive - "The data were analyzed by the researcher." Active - "The researcher analyzed the data."

Verb Tense:

- **Consistent Use of Verb Tenses:**
  - **Guidelines for Consistent Tense Usage:**
    - Maintain a consistent verb tense within a section or paragraph.
      - Example: The study investigates the effects of climate change on biodiversity. The researchers analyze data from multiple regions.

- **Shifting Tenses in Academic Writing:**
  - **Avoid Unnecessary Shifts:**
    - Example: The literature review presents studies on the topic. The researcher conducted an experiment to further explore the phenomenon.

  - **Use Past Tense for Methods and Results:**
    - Example: The participants were randomly assigned to groups, and the data were analyzed using statistical software.

  - **Use Present Tense for Universally True Statements:**

- Example: The introduction outlines the purpose of the study and presents relevant background information.

V

Visual Elements

Tables and Figures:

- **Guidelines for Creating and Formatting:**
  - **Clear and Concise Titles:**
    - Provide informative titles that succinctly describe the content.
      - Example: **Table 1. Demographic Characteristics of Participants**

  - **Column and Row Headings:**
    - Clearly label columns and rows to facilitate understanding.
      - Example:

Participant ID	Age	Gender	Education Level
001	25	Male	Bachelor's

  - **Consistent Formatting:**
    - Maintain consistency in font size, style, and formatting throughout the table.

- Example:

    Table 2. Results of Experimental Conditions

Condition	Mean Score	Standard Deviation
A	23.5	2.0
B	22.1	1.5

Captions and Notes:

- **Guidelines for Writing Captions and Notes:**
  - **Captions:**
    - Include a caption above tables and below figures.
    - Captions should concisely describe the content.
      - Example:

        Figure 3. Relationship between Time Spent Studying and Exam Performance

  - **Notes:**
    - Include explanatory notes below tables or figures, if necessary.
    - Clearly explain abbreviations or symbols used.
      - Example:

        Note. SD = Standard Deviation. *$p < 0.05$.

Definition and Examples:

- **Definition:**
  - Vulnerable populations refer to groups with characteristics that make them more susceptible to harm or exploitation in research.

- **Examples:**
  - Children, pregnant women, individuals with cognitive impairments, refugees, and prisoners are examples of vulnerable populations.

Guidelines for Conducting Research with Vulnerable Populations:

- **Informed Consent:**
  - Clearly explain the nature of the study, risks, and benefits to participants or their legally authorized representatives.

- **Ethical Considerations:**
  - Pay special attention to the ethical implications of the research, ensuring that participants are treated with respect and dignity.

- **Community Involvement:**
    - Involve the community in the research process, ensuring cultural sensitivity and relevance.
        - Example: If working with a refugee population, collaborate with community leaders to understand cultural nuances.

- **Guardian Consent:**
    - Obtain consent from a legal guardian for participants who cannot provide informed consent themselves.
        - Example: When working with minors, obtain parental or guardian consent.

- **Minimize Harm:**
    - Take measures to minimize potential harm or discomfort to vulnerable participants.
        - Example: If researching traumatic experiences, provide resources for counseling and support.

- **Data Privacy:**
    - Safeguard the privacy and confidentiality of participants, especially when dealing with sensitive information.
        - Example: Use anonymized identifiers in research reporting to protect participant identities.

- **Independent Review:**
  - Seek independent ethical review and approval from an institutional review board (IRB) when working with vulnerable populations.

Made in the USA
Monee, IL
06 January 2024